WHAT ARE EXTREME SPORTS?

SPORTS BOOK AGE 8-10

Children's Sports & Outdoors

Speedy Publishing LLC
40 E. Main St. #1156
Newark, DE 19711
www.speedypublishing.com

Extreme sports are sports encompassing the always changing array of sports that typically involve some type of wild tricks, danger, speed, and/or height. Several sports referred to as extreme sports include snowboarding, skateboarding, surfing and BMX.

It is typically the excitement or rush that people enjoy from these sports, not the competition. Each competition typically involves races between competitors or competitions that are judged for the best stunts or tricks. Extreme sports are often considered as non-conventional or newer sports. In this book, you will be learning about some of these activities.

SAFETY FIRST!

Safety should always be a consideration when engaging in any extreme sport. You will still be able to enjoy the rush from landing that amazing trick, or from the high speed, but you must ensure that you understand how to safely perform the sport.

This may be as simple as wearing a helmet, but sometimes it might involve learning from a professional that is trained in the sport. Be sure to have the safety equipment that is recommended for the particular sport you are interested in, be sure that you obtain the correct training, and be sure to always double check your equipment's condition prior to starting the sport. *NOTE: CHILDREN make sure that you obtain permission from your parents and only attempt tricks with the supervision of adults!*

BREATHTAKING BMX BIKER STUNT

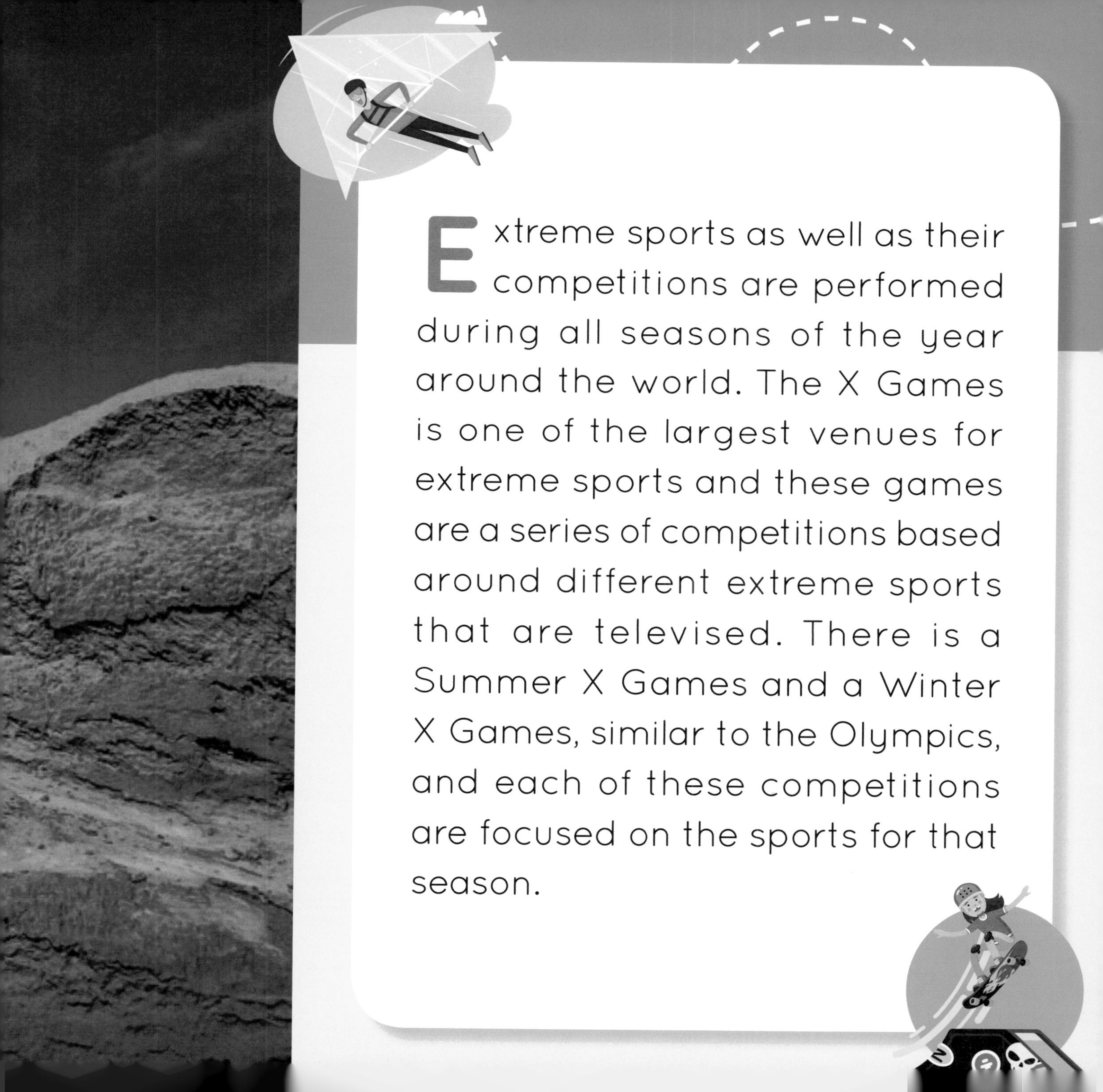

Extreme sports as well as their competitions are performed during all seasons of the year around the world. The X Games is one of the largest venues for extreme sports and these games are a series of competitions based around different extreme sports that are televised. There is a Summer X Games and a Winter X Games, similar to the Olympics, and each of these competitions are focused on the sports for that season.

The Games are held in different cities once a year. Just like the Olympics, they award medals of bronze, silver, and gold for each event.

Summer extreme sports include BMX, In-Line Skating, MotoX, Skateboarding, and Surfing. Winter extreme sports include Skiing, Snowboarding, and Snowmobiling.

BMX BIKES

BMX is an acronym for Bicycle MotorCross which is a bicycling form meant to copy MotorCross motorcycles. There are several types of BMX sports competitions that include stunt and racing BMX; however, it is also considered to be enjoyed by millions as a recreational activity around the world.

BMX BIKER

When riding any kind of bicycle, you should always be wearing a helmet as well as good shoes. In addition to the helmet and good shoes, it is also recommended when you are riding a BMX bike that you wear pads, gloves, and thigh, shin, and arm guards. While this may seem like a lot to be wearing, you have to protect yourself when racing or performing BMX jumps or stunts.

576.

BMX started with BMX racing. Other forms of BMX racing include Flatland, Street and Park, Stunt Vert, and MotoX Motorcross, which is a combination of cross country racing and motorcycle racing.

Becoming one of the Moto X's premier events, the X Games consists of 4 competitive motorcross events that include Freestyle, Best Trick, Supermoto, and Step Up.

SKATEBOARDING

This is a freestyle sport where the only limits are those imposed by the athlete's ability and imagination. Most of the time, it is a recreational activity done at a skateboard part or on the local streets. There is a skateboarding competition judges determine the winner using a points system.

SURFING

Surfing is known as much as a way of life or attitude as it is considered a sport. While there are surfing competitions, it is typically a recreational activity enjoyed by many.

Surfing is a sport that involves using a surfboard to ride ocean waves. A surfer has to swim out into the ocean and lays on the surfboard on his stomach. Once the surfer sees a wave, he aims his board towards land and starts paddling so that he can "catch" the wave.

As the wave starts propelling the surfer, he pops up to stand on the board. The surfer now rides the wave as the board starts speeding towards the shore.

There are tricks that can be performed and they can ride the wave at an angle so they can ride the wave for a longer period of time.

Surfing extreme's side is to catch the largest wave possible. There are times when a surfer will pull themselves farther out in the ocean with a jetski looking for faster and larger waves. This can be a very dangerous sport since the waves can be close and powerful. The largest wave ever surfed is said to be 70 feet tall.

Competition surfing is judged as the competitors ride series of waves and the judges determine who performed the best. The scores are based on several factors that include the tricks performed and the length of the ride.

SNOW SKIING

The most popular and traditional winter sport throughout the world is snow skiing. While it is a popular sport for fun, it is also known as a competitive sport in the Olympics as well as the X Games.

COMPETITIVE SNOW SKIING

Some of the competitive skiing events include the popular events you see at the Olympics that include slalom, downhill, ski jump, and cross country. The cross country, downhill, and slalom are events where the skiers race against each other, but the end goal is to get through the event course in the quickest time.

Recently introduced at the X Games are skiing events such as Skier X and Big Air. Skier X involves a race where the skiers are permitted to bump against each other.

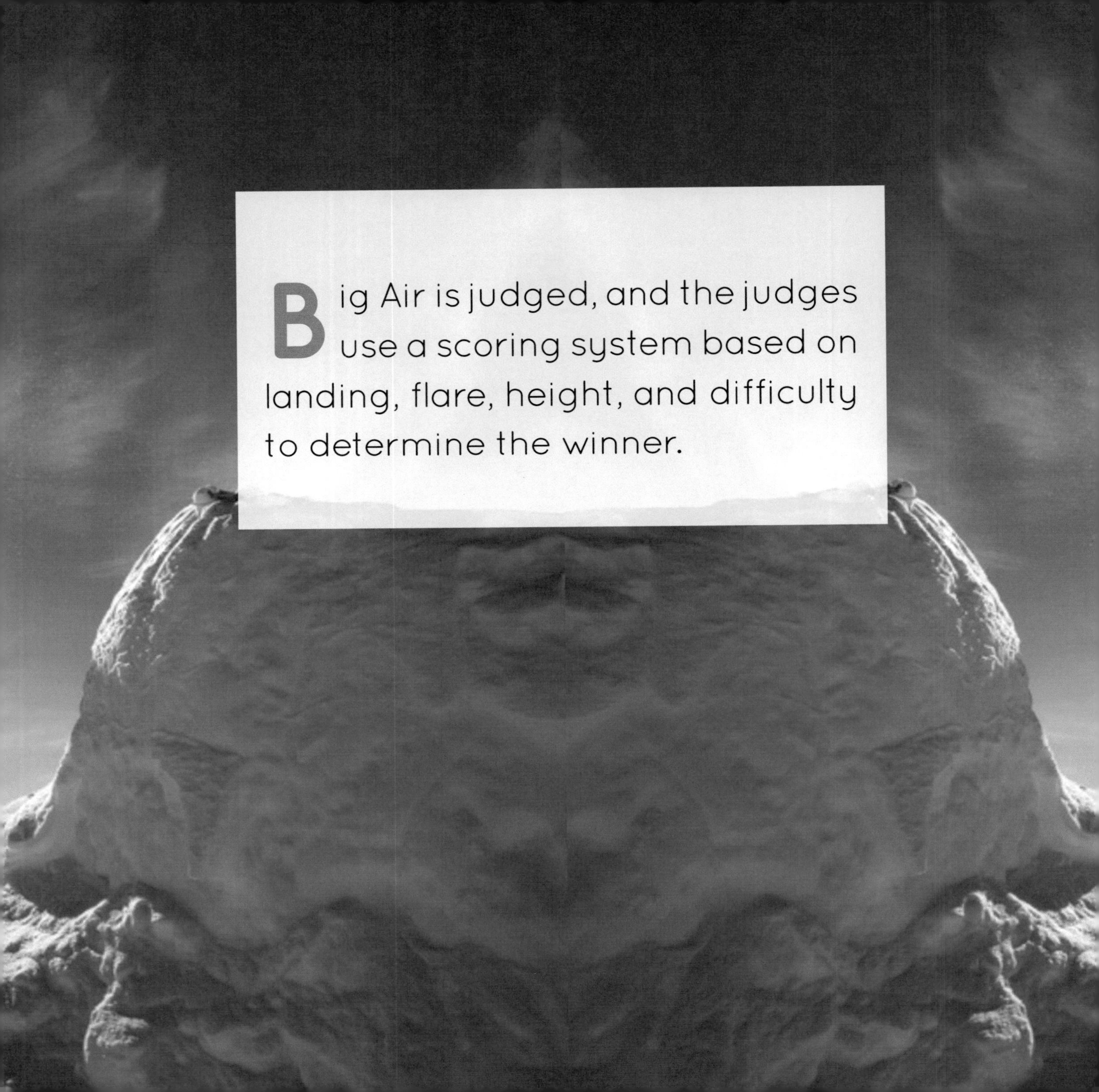

Big Air is judged, and the judges use a scoring system based on landing, flare, height, and difficulty to determine the winner.

BIG AIR JUMP

SPEED SKIING

EXTREME SPEED SKIING

Speed skiing gained momentum during the 90s and involves skiing the fastest downhill in a straight line. This is known as the fastest, non-motorized winter sport around the world. It can be extremely dangerous and should be performed only be trained skiers.

SNOWBOARDING

Snowboarding is an amazing combination of skiing, surfing, and skateboarding. The snowboarder attaches their boots to the snowboard and then slide down some type of snowy slope. This has become a popular sport for winter.

SNOWBOARDER

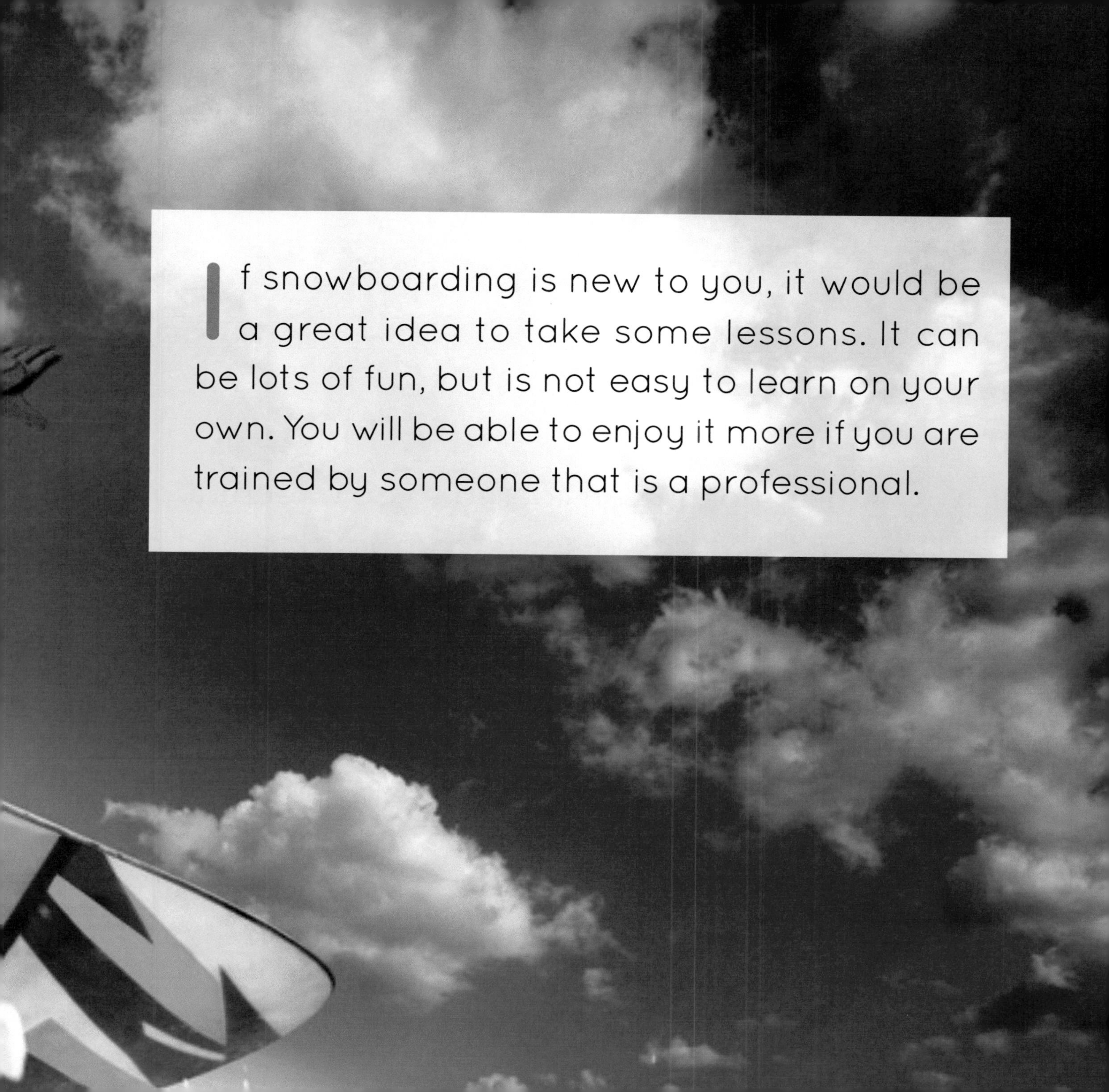

If snowboarding is new to you, it would be a great idea to take some lessons. It can be lots of fun, but is not easy to learn on your own. You will be able to enjoy it more if you are trained by someone that is a professional.

COMPETITIVE SNOWBOARDING

While mostly considered to be a recreational sport, it can also be competitive and has become an Olympic sport. Events at the Olympics include Snowboard Cross, Half-pipe, and the Parallel Giant Slalom.

SKI GATES WITH RED FLAG AND BLUE PARALLEL SLALOM

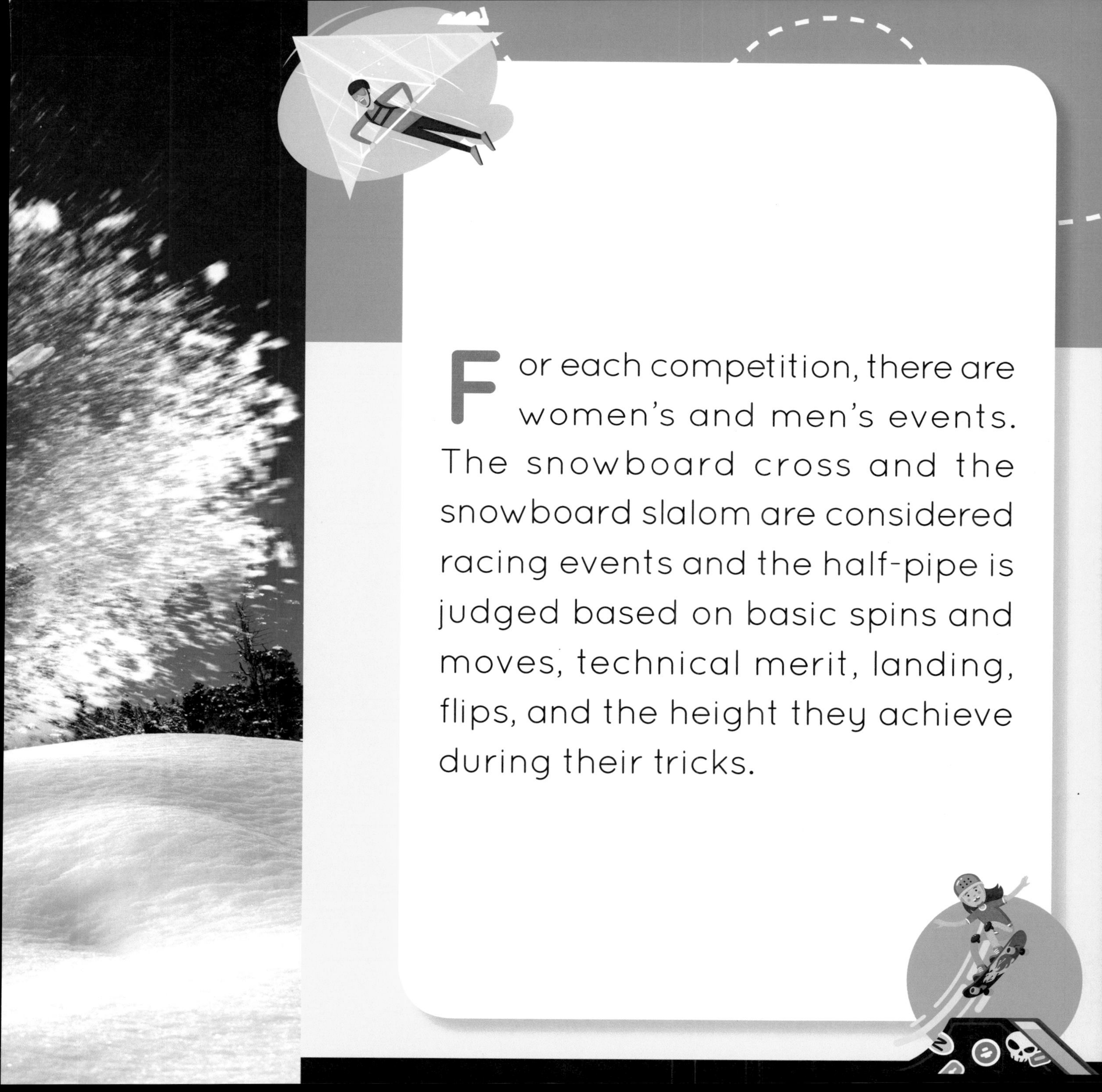

For each competition, there are women's and men's events. The snowboard cross and the snowboard slalom are considered racing events and the half-pipe is judged based on basic spins and moves, technical merit, landing, flips, and the height they achieve during their tricks.

SNOWMOBILING

SNOWMOBILING

A snowmobile is a vehicle propelled by one or two tracks made of rubber and skis used for steering. They are made to drive on ice and snow, and do not need a road or a trail. They are usually large, weighing more than 600 pounds, machines that are very powerful and are operated by a trained driver.

While sometimes they are used simply for transportation, snowmobiles are used mostly for recreation. However, they are also used in several sports and during extreme conditions.

They have the ability to achieve high speeds (up to 90 miles per hour), travel over jumps, as well as travel over water for a short period of time (which is not recommended).

SAFETY FIRST!

Snowmobiles are not meant for use by young children. They are powerful, large machines that can be quite dangerous. You should be trained to operate it and have your parent along for the ride. Each state has different age requirements for operating a snowmobile. Be sure that you know the laws and that you are old enough to drive one.

Safety has to be your first concern when you ride a snowmobile. While the speed and open air of the rice can be very exciting, it can also be very dangerous as it is easy to get tossed from a snowmobile and it can sometimes be difficult to get it to stop, particularly when you are riding on ice. All riders should wear goggles, gloves, a helmet, as well as other protective clothing. It can be easy to get frostbite with the wind and high speeds causing a colder wind chill.

SNOWMOBILE RACE

X GAMES
NAVY

COMPETITIVE SNOWMOBILING

There are two major snowmobiling events in the X Games:

- HillCross is a fun competition to watch where the riders travel up a hill, similar to Skier X or Snowboarder X.
- Soros is a race where the track is part cross country and part oval, and is often referred to as NASCAR on snow. At the same time, several racers race and the winners advance to the next heat.

PLAY EXTREME SPORTS WITH CAUTION

There are many other extreme sports for any weather conditions. Do NOT attempt any of these sports without proper training and the permission of your parents.

To learn about these extreme sports or answer any questions about the sports discussed in this book, you can visit your local library, research the internet, and ask questions of your teachers, family, and friends.

Visit

www.BabyProfessorBooks.com

to download Free Baby Professor eBooks and view our catalog of new and exciting Children's Books

Made in the USA
Thornton, CO
07/15/24 11:47:28

cb39b0de-4690-4cbb-a5f7-6c0d709b3473R01